VIETNAM

Still Struggling, Still Spirited

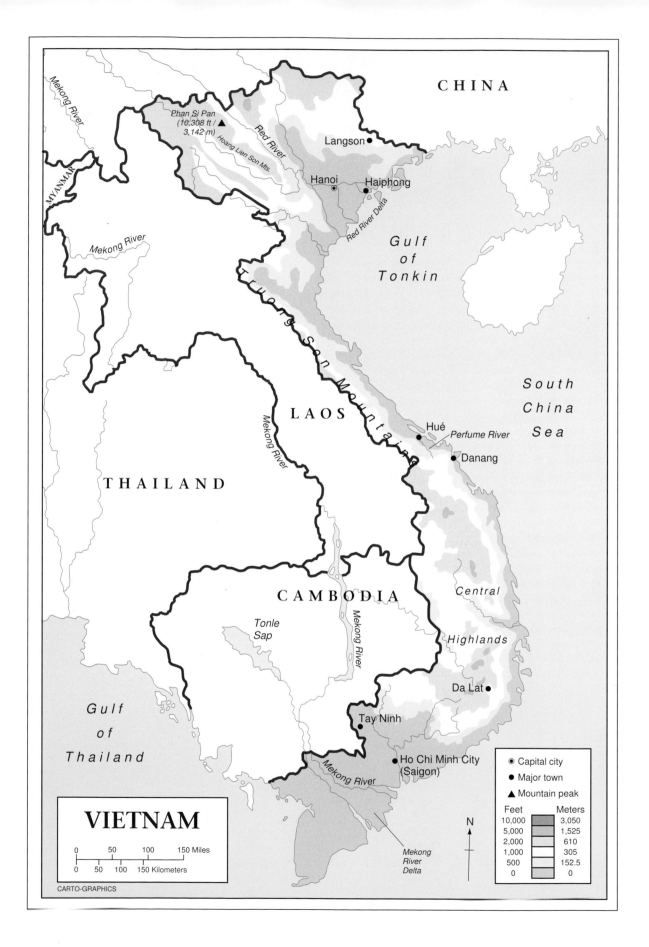

CHINA

Mekong River

Phan Si Pan
(10,308 ft /
3,142 m) ▲

Hoang Lien Son Mts.

Red River

Langson

Mekong River

MYANMAR

Hanoi ⊙ ● Haiphong

Red River Delta

Gulf
of
Tonkin

South
China
Sea

Truong Son Mountains

LAOS

Mekong River

Hué ●
Perfume River

THAILAND

● Danang

Mekong River

CAMBODIA

Tonle
Sap

Mekong River

Central

Highlands

Da Lat ●

Gulf
of
Thailand

Tay Ninh ●

● Ho Chi Minh City
(Saigon)

Mekong River

⊙ Capital city

● Major town

▲ Mountain peak

Mekong
River
Delta

N

VIETNAM

| 0 | 50 | 100 | 150 Miles |
| 0 | 50 | 100 | 150 Kilometers |

Feet	Meters
10,000	3,050
5,000	1,525
2,000	610
1,000	305
500	152.5
0	0

VIETNAM

Still Struggling, Still Spirited

Olivia Skelton

BENCHMARK **B**OOKS

MARSHALL CAVENDISH
NEW YORK

*The publisher would like to thank Keith Weller Taylor,
Associate Professor of Vietnamese Cultural Studies
at Cornell University, for his expert review
of the manuscript.*

Benchmark Books
Marshall Cavendish Corporation
99 White Plains Road
Tarrytown, New York 10591-9001

Library of Congress Cataloging-in-Publication Data
Skelton, Olivia.
    Vietnam: still struggling, still spirited / by Olivia Skelton.
       p.   cm. — (Exploring cultures of the world)
    Includes bibliographical material and index.
    Summary: Describes the geography, history, climate, government, people, and
culture of this small country in the southeastern corner of Asia.
    ISBN 0-7614-0395-7 (lib. bdg.)
    1. Vietnam—Civilization—Juvenile literature. [1. Vietnam.] I. Title. II. Series.
DS556.3.S55   1998
    959.7—dc21   97-8802
                                                           CIP
                                                           AC

Printed in Hong Kong

Series design by Carol Matsuyama

Front cover: A young woman at a *Tet* celebration in Hanoi
Back cover: Colorful decorations for sale at a Hanoi shop

Photo Credits
Front and back covers, title page, and pages 6, 9, 11, 18, 21, 22, 23, 24, 25, 26-27, 28, 30, 32, 33,
34, 36, 37, 39, 42, 45, 46, 49, 52, 54, 56, 57: ©Martha Hess; pages 10 and 51: ©Brent Peters;
page 14: North Wind Picture Archives; page 15: Wide World Photos, Inc.

Contents

The dragon is an ancient symbol that appears in many Vietnamese legends and stories.

1
GEOGRAPHY AND HISTORY

Struggling
to Be Free

Spirits of Mountain and Sea

Long, long, ago, in the land we now call Vietnam, a dragon lord named Lac Long Quan married a fairy spirit named Au Co. They lived happily together in their kingdom for many years and had one hundred sons. Then, one day, Lord Lac Long Quan told his queen that he would have to leave her.

Lac Long Quan took fifty of their sons and traveled east. He set up a kingdom on the green, fertile plains near the sea. Queen Au Co took their other sons west to live in the cool mountain forests.

Lac Long Quan picked one of his sons, Van Lang, to rule his kingdom. Van Lang was the first of eighteen kings.

The eighteenth king had a very beautiful daughter. Word of her beauty spread, and two powerful princes came to him to ask for her hand in marriage. The princes were Son Tinh, the Spirit of the Mountains, and Thuy Tinh, the Spirit of the Waters.

The king could not decide which prince would have the privilege of marrying his daughter. So he created a contest. The prince who would give him the most beautiful gift would marry his daughter. Son Tinh, the Spirit of the Mountains, was the first to present a magnificent gift to the king. So he won the hand of the beautiful princess and took her into the mountains to live.

The Spirit of the Waters, Thuy Tinh, was very angry. He vowed revenge. To punish Son Tinh and his people, he sent powerful waters into the mountains to cause flooding. But Son Tinh was powerful, too. He drove the waters out of the mountains and back to the sea.

Legend says that the two main groups of people in today's Vietnam—the Vietnamese of the lowlands in the east and the mountain peoples of the west and north—sprang from these roots. So did the conflict between them. The descendants of Lord Lac Long Quan have tried for years to dominate the people of the mountains. The descendants of Queen Au Co have tried for just as long to resist and maintain their own way of life in the mountains. Some might say that the spirits of Thuy Tinh and Son Tinh continue their struggle.

A Pole with a Rice Basket at Each End

Vietnam lies in the southeastern corner of Asia, curving like a twisting dragon along the eastern edge of the Indochina Peninsula. Compared to the United States, Vietnam is small. It is only slightly bigger than the state of New Mexico. But it has many people—more than 75 million.

The country is broad in the north and south and narrow in the center. The Vietnamese compare this shape to a carrying tool called a *don ganh*. This is a long bamboo pole with baskets for carrying rice at both ends. The "baskets" of Vietnam are two wide rice-growing lowlands, where most people live. The one in the north is the Red River Delta. The one in the south is the Mekong River Delta. (A delta is an area of land at the mouth of a river.) The "pole," or the long narrow center of the *don ganh,* is formed by the rugged hills of the Central Highlands and the Truong Son Mountains.

As they have been for centuries, the waterways of the Mekong Delta are still used to transport the region's products.

Land of Mountains, Rain Forests, and Seashores

Vietnam is a land of rough mountains, dense forests, and tropical seashores. This beautiful country extends along the east coast of the Indochina Peninsula, bordered by the South China Sea and the Gulf of Tonkin.

Most of the country is mountainous. The Truong Son mountain range fills the western part of the country. It runs along Vietnam's border with Laos and Cambodia. The higher peaks of the Hoang Lien Son Mountains dot the border with China in the north.

In central Vietnam, swift rivers tumble out of the Central Highlands on their way to the sea, forming waterfalls and deep ravines. Some highlands reach the coast in steep cliffs and seaside hills. Along the coast stretch white, sandy beaches.

Vietnam's highlands were once covered by lush rain forests.

Rain forests once covered much of Vietnam's highlands. Today, only about one-fourth of the original forest remains. Loggers have cut many of Vietnam's valuable tropical trees. Farmers have also cut many trees to clear land for crops or firewood. In the 1960s and 1970s, when Vietnam was at war, acres of trees were killed by chemicals, which were sprayed to uncover the hideouts of soldiers.

In the 1980s, the people of Vietnam began to reforest many areas. Soldiers and children planted millions of trees. These trees now cover many acres of land.

Blowing Hot and Cold

Northern and southern Vietnam have different climates. Most of the north has two seasons: a dry and cool winter and a wet, hot summer. Some areas of the far north, though, have four seasons. The southern lowland is warm and humid all year long. At higher elevations throughout the country the climate is cooler, and there is more rain.

Because of monsoons—seasonal winds that sweep over the Indian Ocean and southern Asia and bring rains— Vietnam is very wet. Most parts of the country get at least 32 inches (81 centimeters) of rainfall each year. Many places receive much more. From April through October the winds of the summer monsoon blow from the southwest and bring warm, humid weather to most of Vietnam.

During the fall, the winds change direction. From November through March, the winds of the winter monsoon

Although most rice is grown in the lowlands, there are some rice fields in the highlands, such as this one in northwestern Vietnam.

blow in from the northeast. They bring wet, chilly weather to northern and central Vietnam.

Between July and November, violent storms called typhoons strike Vietnam. They often cause terrible flooding that destroys crops and homes.

Vietnam has many different types of vegetation. Dwarf bamboo trees and needle trees grow in the mountains of the northwest. In the far south, tropical fruit trees, palms, and mangrove forests flourish.

Vietnam has a great variety of wildlife. There are fifty species of mammals, including elephants, rhinoceroses, and tigers. Reptile species include crocodiles and large snakes like the python. Vietnam also has more than 600 species of birds. The government has set aside several large areas of land, called reserves, to protect endangered species.

The Struggle to Create a Country

For thousands of years, the people of Vietnam have had to fight off invaders. The Chinese have swept down from the north again and again, taking control, getting driven out, then taking control again. But the Chinese have not been the only invaders. Mongols, Indians, Portuguese, British, French, Japanese, and Americans have all fought to control Vietnam.

Fighting to protect their homeland has given the Vietnamese a strong sense of nationhood. Some of the country's most celebrated heroes are people who have led battles to free their homeland from invaders.

Vietnam's roots are in the Red River Delta of the north. Historians believe that groups of Viet people originally moved there from lands to the south. For a long time, they lived independently in small farming villages. But around

100 B.C., China took control. The Vietnamese rebelled against the Chinese several times. Two female warriors, the Trung sisters, led one of the most famous rebellions. They chased the Chinese back across the border in approximately A.D. 40. But two years later the Chinese regained control. They ruled the Vietnamese in the Red River Delta for 900 years.

The Vietnamese finally ended Chinese control around the year 938. Vietnamese emperors then ruled for many years. By 1471, the Vietnamese had conquered the Kingdom of Champa, in what is now central Vietnam. In the 1600s, they added lands of the Khmer, near Saigon (now called Ho Chi Minh City), and the Mekong Delta. By the 1700s, the Vietnamese controlled most of what we now call Vietnam.

Invaders from Across the Sea

In the 1400s, European explorers traveled to Asia. They returned home with tales of Asian lands overflowing with spices, silks, and gems. Many Europeans dreamed of getting rich through trade with Asia. Missionaries also dreamed of going to Asia, to convert people to Christianity.

The Portuguese arrived on the Vietnamese coast in 1516 and set up a trading post. Dutch, British, and French traders followed. By the 1700s, the French were the largest group of European settlers in Vietnam. In order to protect them and their businesses, French soldiers were stationed in Vietnam. Conflicts between the French and the Vietnamese grew.

At that time Vietnam was weak. As they expanded south, the rulers in the north had found it harder to maintain control. Local warlords were in power in many areas. As the Vietnamese were busy fighting one another, European powers like France gained greater control.

French forces attack the village of Langson in north Vietnam.

In the 1860s, the French conquered the far south around Saigon, but did not take over the north until the 1880s. By 1883, France controlled the whole country. Then, in 1885, Vietnam signed a peace treaty accepting French control. The Vietnamese emperor stayed on his throne, but France ruled.

Fighting for Independence

Life was difficult for the Vietnamese under French rule. Many poor Vietnamese farmers were forced off their land to make room for French rubber plantations. The Vietnamese worked for low pay under harsh conditions. They were not allowed to hold the best jobs or high public office in their own country.

Resentment against the French grew. By the early 1900s, several groups had formed to fight for independence.

Although acts of rebellion took place, Vietnam's best chance to break away didn't come until World War II (1939–1945). After Germany invaded France in 1940, the French continued to govern Vietnam, but under Japanese supervision. Japan was Germany's ally.

During the Japanese occupation, one of Vietnam's most celebrated leaders, Ho Chi Minh, began the fight for independence. Ho had left Vietnam after high school to work and travel abroad. He returned in 1939 to organize a group of resistance fighters called the Viet Minh.

After Germany and Japan lost the war, the Viet Minh declared Vietnam independent. The French tried to hold on to Vietnam by force. A long war between France and Vietnam followed. It finally ended, on May 7, 1954, when the French surrendered.

A peace treaty was signed a few months later. It divided Vietnam "temporarily" into two countries. The Viet Minh and their allies controlled the "Democratic Republic of Vietnam" in the north. The French and their allies controlled the "Republic of Vietnam" in the south.

Elections were planned for July 20, 1956. The country was then to be united under a new leader. But the elections never took place.

Ho Chi Minh was a leader in Vietnam's fight for independence.

15

Thinking that Ho would win the elections, the leaders in the south refused to go through with them. The leaders of the north felt cheated and promised to reunite their country.

War between North and South

Full-scale war broke out between north and south in 1959. By that time, the French were gone and the United States was getting involved. The United States and its allies supported the south, many of whose people were against communism. China and the Soviet Union (Russia) supported Ho and the northern forces, who were Communist.

At first, the United States sent only small groups of what it called "advisers" to Vietnam. American involvement gradually increased. By the late 1960s, there were 500,000 U.S. soldiers in Vietnam.

Thousands of American soldiers died in the Vietnam War, which became very unpopular in the United States. Protests from the American people helped to convince the U.S. government to reduce the number of soldiers in Vietnam.

Lacking the support it needed from the United States, South Vietnam quickly lost the war. North Vietnam captured Saigon, the capital of South Vietnam, in April 1975. On July 2, 1976, the North Vietnamese declared Vietnam unified, as the new "Socialist Republic of Vietnam." Many supporters of South Vietnam left the country. Since then, several hundred thousand Vietnamese have settled in the United States.

As a result of the Vietnam War, 3 million Vietnamese were killed and 4 million were wounded. More than half the people of Vietnam were left homeless, and much of the country was destroyed by bombs and chemical weapons. More than 58,000 Americans were killed or are still missing.

VIETNAMESE GOVERNMENT

Vietnam is a Communist state. This means that, although there is a National Assembly, a president, and a prime minister, the Communist Party makes all important decisions. A group called the Politburo heads Vietnam's Communist Party. The Politburo has fifteen members.

The National Assembly has 395 members. They are elected every five years. The National Assembly meets several times a year to approve laws made by the Communist Party.

The National Assembly also picks a person to serve a five-year term as president. The president is the head of state, but his duties are mainly ceremonial. Vietnam's president selects the prime minister, who actually runs the government with the approval of the Politburo.

People who are eighteen years of age or older must vote in Vietnam. But no one can run for public office without government approval.

A New Vietnam

For many years after the war, Vietnam had little contact with non-Communist countries. Conditions in Vietnam were difficult. Much of the country was in ruins. People were poor. Food and other goods were scarce. The Communist Party had strict control over the people.

Finally, in 1986, the leaders of Vietnam announced their plan for improving things. This plan was called *doi moi*, which means "change to the new." Vietnam opened trade with many non-Communist countries. In addition, the government began allowing more foreigners to start businesses in Vietnam, and encouraged people of other nations to visit and spend money in Vietnam.

Because of *doi moi*, life in Vietnam is getting better. Relations with other countries are improving, too. In 1994, the United States and Vietnam established diplomatic relations for the first time since the end of the Vietnam War.

17

Most people of Vietnam are ethnic Vietnamese. They are descendants of the Viet people who originally settled in northern Vietnam.

2
THE PEOPLE

Who Are the Vietnamese?

Vietnam is an ancient nation. Its people can trace their roots back thousands of years. About 90 percent of the population are "ethnic Vietnamese."

The ethnic Vietnamese are descendants of the Viet people who originally settled in the Red River Valley. Over the centuries, they spread south to occupy all the lowlands of modern Vietnam.

The remaining 10 percent of Vietnam's population is made up of some 52 minority groups. Some of their ancestors reached Vietnam long ago, as conquerors, traders, or colonists. Others are descendants of people the Vietnamese conquered as they moved south from the Red River.

Many of Vietnam's minority groups live in the Central Highlands and in the remote mountains of the north. All together, they number several million people. Each group has its own distinct language and way of life.

More than 1 million Chinese live in Vietnam. Mostly, they reside in a part of Ho Chi Minh City called Cholon. (Saigon was renamed Ho Chi Minh City by the Communists when they came to power.) Because of bad treatment by the

Vietnamese, however, many Chinese have left Vietnam during the last few years.

There are about 700,000 Khmer (Cambodians) in Vietnam. They are descendants of the people of the Khmer Empire, which once covered what is now southern Vietnam.

About 100,000 Chams also live in the country. Their ancestors once ruled the Kingdom of Champa, in what is now central Vietnam. After the Vietnamese defeated them in the 1400s, many Chams fled to the highlands, where they joined upland groups. Today, Chams live in Ho Chi Minh City and in several provinces in lowland or coastal areas.

A Crowded Land

There are about 76 million people in Vietnam, making it the thirteenth most populous country in the world. It is also the most densely populated country in Southeast Asia.

Because Vietnam is a poor country with a large population, the government encourages families to have just two children. So far, this policy has failed. Vietnamese families have an average of four children, so the nation's population is still growing. One reason families continue to have more than two children is that, on the farms, where most people live, many hands are needed to do the work. Children provide needed labor.

Most Vietnamese people live along the crowded lowland areas of the coast and in the deltas of the Red and Mekong Rivers. The government is trying to redistribute the population through what it calls a "resettlement" program, in order to ease crowding. Under this program, several million people have been moved from densely populated areas to less crowded ones.

Many villagers, such as these banana sellers in Hanoi, come to the cities to sell their crops.

Making a Living

Most Vietnamese are farmers. They grow rice or other crops such as sweet potatoes, melons, bananas, oranges, sugarcane, tea, and coffee. Some people raise chickens, ducks, or pigs to make extra money. Many people in coastal areas earn their living by fishing.

In the cities, people have many of the same jobs held by people in cities all over the world. They are office and factory workers, artists, shopkeepers, doctors, teachers, bus drivers, and government officials.

The Vietnamese are early risers. On farms, the day starts before dawn. Even in cities, people are up and about by

21

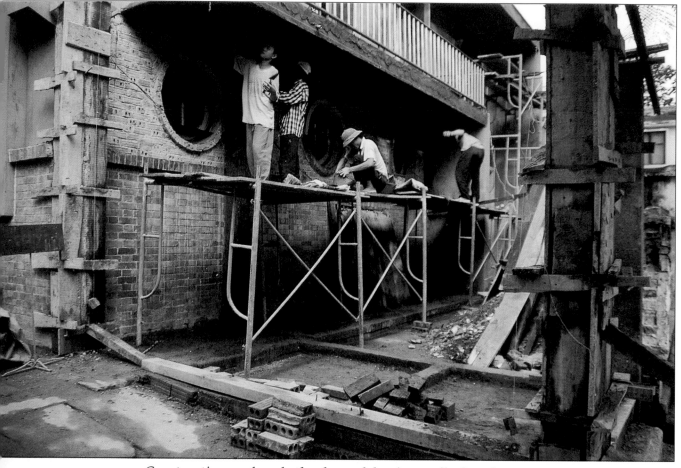

Construction work and other heavy labor is usually done by men.

5:30 A.M. Work in the cities starts at about 7:00 A.M. Everyone stops for lunch at about 11:00 A.M. They return to work two hours later.

Work usually ends at 4:00 P.M. For many people, however, the workday is not over then, for they must take a second job to make ends meet. The Vietnamese often work six days a week.

Because many Vietnamese men died during the Vietnam War, many of the workers today are women. They do every kind of work, but men still hold most positions of authority.

From Countryside to City

Although Vietnam has several large cities, 80 percent of the people live in the countryside. Villages in northern and central Vietnam contain several houses surrounded by a border of bamboo trees. In the center of the village, a Buddhist temple serves as both a house of worship and a community center. In southern Vietnam, houses are lined up along the main roads or canals. Houses along rivers in the Mekong Delta are built on stilts to help withstand floods.

This house in the Mekong Delta rests on stilts. The stilts raise the house high above the nearby river and help keep it dry when the river floods.

Workers replace the straw roof on a house in the country.

Most rural houses are made of wood, straw, and bamboo. Some are made of clay bricks. Most houses lack running water and electricity.

In the Central Highlands and the mountains of the far north, people often live in long, narrow houses with thatched roofs. Some houses are raised so they are far enough off the ground to prevent the entry of animals and snakes. As in the rest of Vietnam, several generations of a family often live in one house.

About 20 percent of Vietnam's people live in cities. Most of them have small, cramped apartments near where they work. By 6:00 A.M., city parks are full of people doing exercises. By 6:30, the streets are full of traffic. City peddlers cram sidewalks with stands and pushcarts selling breakfast.

Vietnam's Bustling Cities

Ho Chi Minh City is Vietnam's largest city, with a population of more than 5 million. The city was originally named Saigon but was renamed Ho Chi Minh City in 1975. Most people, though, still call it Saigon.

Many people ride bicycles and motorbikes to get around in Ho Chi Minh City.

Ho Chi Minh City is Vietnam's center of business, banking, manufacturing, and trade. It is Vietnam's wealthiest and most international city. Many downtown streets are lined with elegant restaurants, newly remodeled office buildings, and large hotels. Cars are no longer as rare in Ho Chi Minh City as they once were. But the city streets are still crowded with people on bicycles and motorbikes. Western influence in music, clothing, and language is greater here than in other parts of Vietnam. It isn't unusual to see young people wearing jeans and T-shirts or listening to the latest rock music from a personal stereo player.

Hanoi, with a population of about 4 million people, is Vietnam's second largest city. It is also the nation's capital and the home of many government and Communist Party officials.

Ho Chi Minh City, with its wide streets and fine buildings, is the commercial center of Vietnam.

A shopper gets off her bike to examine the merchandise on display outside a store in Hanoi.

Like Ho Chi Minh City, Hanoi's streets are bustling with bicycles and motor scooters. Hanoi also has its share of street merchants. From them, people can get a haircut, buy a bowl of soup, or have a bicycle repaired.

In Hanoi, the French built many grand houses along wide, tree-shaded boulevards. The houses are made of stucco, a cement-like material. They have tile roofs and wide porches. Hanoi also has some of the country's best museums. But many of the oldest buildings in Hanoi are now run-down.

Vietnam has several other large cities, such as Haiphong, Danang, and Hué. All of these lie on or near the coast.

Most of the goods that enter and leave northern Vietnam pass through Haiphong, a port 63 miles (100 kilometers) east of Hanoi on the Gulf of Tonkin. Haiphong is an industrial city with factories that make bricks, glass, cement, and textiles. It is also a shipbuilding center.

Danang is a major port on the coast of central Vietnam. In Danang, many people like to visit the Cham Museum. It contains the world's largest collection of sandstone carvings from the Kingdom of Champa, which flourished in central and southern Vietnam between the A.D. 100s and 1400s.

Hué is Vietnam's educational, religious, and cultural center. It is a beautiful city, located on the Perfume River north of Danang. Hué is famous for its many lovely pagodas (the

VIETNAMESE NAMES

Vietnamese people write their family name first, then their middle name, and then their first name. This is opposite to the way people write their names in North America. Titles such as "Mr." and "Mrs." are applied to the first name, not the last, as in "Mrs. Mary."

The title used before a person's name depends partly on his or her age. For example, "Mr." is *Ong* if the man is of your grandparents' age, *Bac* if the man is of your parents' age, *Chu* if the man is younger than your parents, and *Anh* if the man is in his teens or early twenties. "Mrs." is *Ba* if the woman is of your grandparents' age, and *Bac* if she is of your parents' age or younger. "Miss" is *Em* or *Chi*, unless the woman is very young, in which case it's *Co*.

Girls are often named after rivers, birds, or flowers. Common girls' names include Phuong ("fragrance") and Hoa ("flower"). Boys are usually given names that signify some personal quality. Common names for boys include Duc ("virtue") and Khiem ("modesty").

At home, parents often call their children ugly names to keep evil spirits away from them. For example, a child might be called "cow" or "bear"!

The family name Nguyen is very popular in Vietnam. In fact, about half of the people in Vietnam have this name. There are few different family names in Vietnam because many years ago people often changed their family name to that of the emperor. The name Nguyen is popular because the Nguyen family ruled during the last empire. Other common family names are Tran, Le, Phan, and Ngo.

A fishing net is stretched between poles on the Perfume River in Hué.

towers of Buddhist temples), which dot the landscape. The Royal Citadel, a huge brick fortress where Vietnamese emperors once lived, is also located in Hué. Fighting during the Vietnam War destroyed most of the Royal Citadel, but the front gate and some of the smaller buildings inside still stand.

Language of Many Tones

The Vietnamese language is closely related to Mon-Khmer, the language of Cambodia. But many of its words come from Chinese and other languages of Southeast Asia.

In Vietnamese, words have different meanings depending on the tone of voice in which they are said. There are six tones in the north and five in the south. So every word can be pronounced in several ways and have several meanings. For example, the word *ma* can mean "phantom," "mother," "rice seedling," "tomb," "horse," or "but"—depending on the tone used to say it!

In written Vietnamese, accent marks over or under letters show the tones. Every syllable is a separate word, so the Vietnamese write Saigon as "Sai Gon" and Vietnam as "Viet Nam."

SAY IT IN VIETNAMESE

Because Vietnamese is a tonal language, the meaning of a word changes depending on the tone used by the speaker. Marks placed over or under words indicate tones:

- A line above a letter rising from left to right, as in *á*, means a rising tone.
- A line above a letter falling from left to right, as in *à*, means a falling tone.
- A mark that looks like a question mark, as in *ả*, means a tone that starts low, falls slightly, then rises.
- A mark above a letter that looks like a wavy line, as in *ã*, means a tone that starts high, dips a bit, then rises quickly again.
- A dot underneath a letter, as in *ạ*, means a low tone that falls and ends suddenly.
- A word with no markings means an even tone said in a normal voice

The Vietnamese language is pronounced differently in the north and south. Many words, such as "yes," also differ in the two regions. The pronunciations and words given below are from the north.

Now, see how you do with the words and phrases below:

Hello	*Xin chào* (Sin chow)
Good-bye	*Tạm biệt* (Tom BEE-it)
Yes	*Vang* (Vahng)
No	*Không* (Khom)
How are you?	*Mạnh giỏi không?* (Mahn zoy khom)
Thank you	*Cảm ón* (Kam un)
You're welcome.	*Không có gì.* (Khom kaw zi)
Excuse me.	*Xin lỗi.* (Sin loy)
What is your name?	*Tên là gì?* (Ten la zi)
My name is _____.	*Tên tôi là.* (Ten toy la)

Although most people in Vietnam speak Vietnamese, more than 55 other languages are spoken by minority groups, such as the Chinese, the Cham, and the Khmer. Many educated Vietnamese also speak French, English, or Russian.

Religion in Vietnam

Most of the people of Vietnam are Buddhists. Buddhism is based on the teaching of the Buddha, a man who lived in India 2,500 years ago. Buddhism first came to Vietnam from China nearly 2,000 years ago. Buddhist temples are common in Vietnam, and many people have small altars in their homes or places of business. Worshipers often burn incense and bring offerings of fruit or flowers to these altars.

Confucianism also has a great influence on the way the Vietnamese live, although it is not really a religion. Confucianism is a philosophy that follows the lessons of Confucius,

Offerings of fruit and flowers adorn a Buddhist altar that has been set up in honor of Tet, the New Year celebration.

The worshipers at this temple in southern Vietnam belong to the Cao Dai faith, one of the religions practiced in Vietnam.

a teacher who lived in China 2,500 years ago. It teaches the importance of respect for authority and lays down rules for a person's duty to family, ancestors, and community. Because of Confucianism, most Vietnamese homes have an honored place for pictures of relatives. People pray to their ancestors for protection and guidance. Families hold ceremonies to honor them on the anniversaries of their deaths.

Other religions that are practiced in Vietnam include Taoism, Roman Catholicism, Cao Dai, Hoa Hao, and Islam. Many of the mountain tribal people practice animism. Animists believe that everything in nature—rocks, trees, bodies of water, and animals—has a spirit. These objects and their spirits must be respected and worshiped.

When the Communists took over Vietnam in 1975, they tried to keep people from practicing their religions. Some of those limitations have since been lifted.

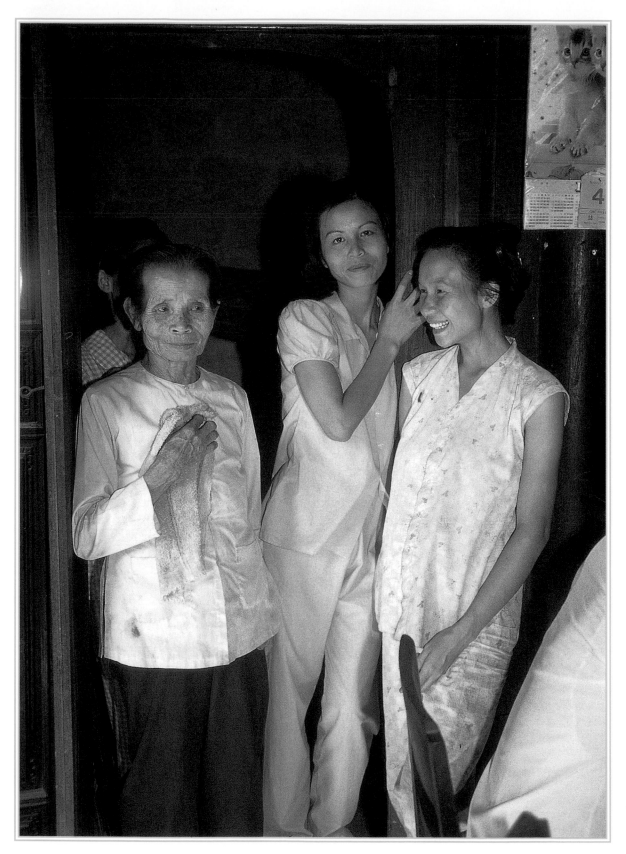

In Vietnam, several generations of one family often live together.

3

FAMILY LIFE, FESTIVALS, AND FOOD

The Vietnamese
Way of Life

In Vietnam, life centers around the family. Every family member has his or her place, depending on gender, age, and birth order. It is a way of life that has lasted for thousands of years. Only now is it starting to change.

Family Customs

North Americans and Europeans often think of the family as consisting of just parents and their children. Vietnamese families also include grandparents—as well as aunts, uncles, and cousins. Many generations often live together in these extended families.

Respect is important in the family. The rules of people in authority—fathers, grandfathers, or eldest sons—may not be questioned. In fact, it is thought to be very disrespectful to disagree with them.

In Vietnam, the man is the head of the household. His wife and children usually obey him in family matters. Women almost never have authority over men. Girls obey their fathers. And women obey their husbands. If a husband dies, the oldest son becomes head of the household.

There are also strict rules about how young men and women behave with each other. If a young woman goes out with a young man, an older person goes along as a chaperone.

At Home

Most Vietnamese homes are small, with little furniture. People often use straw mats for sitting and sleeping. Kitchens that are separate from living areas are rare. In apartments, food is often cooked on small, three-legged stoves that burn wood or coal. Meals are eaten while sitting on the floor or on low chairs around a low table.

During harvest time, the whole family works together in the rice fields.

Women in Vietnam buy most of their fresh fruits and vegetables every day at bustling, open-air markets.

The pace is slow in the countryside. It centers on the seasonal cycle of planting and harvesting crops. Everyone pitches in. Men do heavy work, like plowing or digging irrigation canals. Women help with the planting, weeding, and harvesting. Elderly people tend fruit trees or clean fish ponds. Children work as well. Girls help prepare food, clean house, wash clothes, and tend the vegetable garden. Boys fetch water, take care of farm animals, and help their fathers and older brothers farm or fish. Everyone works as a team on large projects such as building houses.

In cities, work and shopping take up much of the day, especially for women. Not many people have refrigerators, so women visit open-air markets to buy vegetables, fish, or meat each day before or after work. Women also do the cooking. Families gather at about 6:30 P.M. for dinner. A night spent watching television is rare because most families don't have sets. People who do have TVs are likely to have lots of company as neighbors gather around to watch. Most people are in bed by 10:00 or 11:00 P.M.

Holidays and Celebrations

The most important holiday in Vietnam is the lunar New Year, or *Tet*. This holiday is celebrated some time between late January and mid-February. Since it is based on the lunar calendar, the date changes from year to year. The *Tet* festival began thousands of years ago, when farmers held celebrations to thank the gods for the arrival of spring and to pray for a good crop in the new year. The Vietnamese believe that the spirits of their ancestors return to earth at *Tet*. The people sweep graves and decorate home altars with flowers, fresh fruit, and incense to honor visiting spirits. Offices and schools close for three days, but most people celebrate for an entire week.

The Vietnamese welcome the New Year at midnight with the banging of drums and gongs. People dress in their best clothes to visit family and friends. A family's first visitor is very important because he or she will determine the family's luck for the year. A person who has had good fortune is a welcome first guest. But a man or woman whose father has recently died, for example, would be considered bad luck. Feasting is a big part of *Tet*. People enjoy eating special treats

People in Hanoi celebrate Tet *with a festive outdoor dragon display. The dragon is a symbol of strength and fertility in Vietnam.*

such as fried watermelon seeds, sweetened dried fruit, pickled vegetables, sticky sweet rice, pastries wrapped in banana leaves, and candies.

Another one of the many festivals held throughout Vietnam is *Hai Ba Trung.* This is a day in March that celebrates two of Vietnam's most beloved heroes: the Trung sisters, the warriors who chased the Chinese out of Vietnam nearly 2,000 years ago. Villagers in several parts of Vietnam celebrate this holiday. In each village, two girls dress up as the sisters, appearing in colorful costumes. They ride an elephant down the street at the head of a parade.

Tet Trung Thu is a mid-September harvest festival. It is called the Children's Festival because children play such a big part in the celebration. The moon is always full at the time of *Tet Trung Thu*, and the festival is celebrated under its bright glow. Children gather for a parade after dark. They carry colorful lanterns made of rice paper and bamboo. The lanterns are shaped like fish, toads, unicorns, dragons, or stars. Each lantern has a candle inside, which makes it glow as the children carry it through the dark streets to the beat of drums and cymbals. After the celebration, children look forward to eating "moon cakes" made of sticky rice.

The birthdays of new babies are important celebrations in Vietnam. The first birthday celebration occurs when the baby is one month old. The second occurs when the baby is one year old. Family members bring toys, clothing, and money. After age one, people in Vietnam don't celebrate the day when they were born. Instead, everyone celebrates his or her birthday during *Tet*.

The Vietnamese Table

Vietnamese food changes from region to region. Chinese influence is strongest in the north. Cooks use few spices, but stir-fried dishes and soups are popular. The food of central Vietnam can be hot and spicy. Dried chili is a popular seasoning there. Cooks in the south use lots of fresh tropical vegetables, fruits, and herbs. Food is spicy, with tasty curries showing the influence of India.

In Vietnam, eating is a group affair. Bowls of rice and other foods are placed on the table. Diners first fill their bowls from the big rice dish. They then use their chopsticks to pick out pieces of vegetables, fish, or meat from the other bowls

VIETNAMESE CUSTARD

The Vietnamese don't usually end meals with rich or fancy desserts. They're more likely to have fresh fruit. But, if you'd like to try a Vietnamese dessert, this custard dish is popular:

Ingredients:

3 cups fresh or canned coconut milk	3 eggs
1 1/2 cups sugar	3 egg yolks
1/4 cup water	1 teaspoon vanilla

1. Combine 1 cup of the sugar and the water in a saucepan. Cover and place over medium heat for about 4 minutes. Remove the cover and continue cooking about 8 minutes longer as the syrup mixture turns light brown. Stir the mixture as it cooks.

2. Pour the syrup into a 2-quart metal baking pan or mold. Swirl it so that the syrup coats the bottom and the sides of the pan up to 1/3 from the top. Set aside.

3. Beat the whole eggs and egg yolks in a bowl with a fork. Stir in the remaining 1/2 cup sugar, the coconut milk, and the vanilla.

4. Pour the mixture into the baking pan and cover the pan with foil. Put the pan into a larger pan and fill the larger pan with warm water until the water reaches about halfway up the outside of the baking dish containing the custard.

5. Bake for about 1 hour at 350° F. Check the water while the custard bakes. If it starts to boil, lower the temperature slightly, then raise it again to maintain oven temperature. The custard is done when a knife stuck into it near the edge comes out almost clean.

6. When the custard is done, remove it from its water bath. Take off the foil and let it cool slightly before serving.

7. To serve, run a knife around the inside of the pan to loosen the custard. Cover the top of the pan with a plate. Flip the pan and plate over so that the custard falls onto the plate. Lift off the pan. The warm syrup that coated the pan will coat the outside of the custard and run onto the serving dish. Spoon the syrup over pieces of custard as you serve them.

On a crowded city sidewalk, people stop for a delicious lunch of rice, meat, and vegetables.

and place them on the rice. Instead of leaving their bowls on the table, it is usual for diners to hold their bowls of food up to their mouths while they eat.

Rice is part of almost every meal in Vietnam. It is served plain or is sweetened with coconut. It is stirred into soups or fried with vegetables or meat. People grind it into flour and use it to make buns and rice paper. Rice paper is a thin pastry dough used to wrap meat or vegetables. Vietnamese egg rolls are meat and vegetables rolled in rice paper and fried until they are crispy.

Rice is an ingredient in another important Vietnamese food: noodles. These rice noodles might be fried, stuffed in egg rolls, or stir-fried with meat and vegetables. Most Vietnamese begin their day with a breakfast noodle soup called *pho*. The soup contains rice noodles with beef broth, ginger, cinnamon, and small pieces of beef or chicken.

The Vietnamese eat fish, shellfish (such as shrimp), pork, or duck more often than they eat beef. These are served in small pieces so they can be eaten with chopsticks.

A VIETNAMESE WEDDING

Weddings are big family celebrations in Vietnam. In the past, families arranged marriages for their children. Today, young men and women are allowed to choose their own mates. But a man must still ask a woman's father for permission to marry her.

Some Vietnamese couples, especially outside the cities, still get married in the traditional way. In this type of wedding, an older husband and wife, who are the matchmakers, plan the wedding. The groom's family and friends meet at the bride's house. There, the men drink wine and the women chew slices of the bitter-tasting betel nut, wrapped in leaves. The matchmakers light two red candles at the family's altar before the bride and groom exchange wedding rings. They then tie the hands of the couple together with pink thread. This is a symbol of the happiness they hope to share. Next, the bride and groom eat a piece of ginseng root dipped in salt. The bitter taste symbolizes the problems that may come in the future. The matchmakers then pronounce the couple married, and everyone goes to the groom's house to eat and celebrate.

These days, most couples no longer get married in this way. Instead they have a wedding ceremony that takes place over two days. On the first day, the groom, his parents, and a group of family members go to the bride's house to ask for her father's permission to marry. The groom makes a present of betel leaves to the bride's family. Then the bride's family consults its ancestors at the family altar.

With formal permission granted, the marriage ceremony occurs on the second day. It is a solemn ceremony performed at an altar set up at the groom's house. Rituals, such as asking the blessings of spirits, drinking cups of rice alcohol, eating ginger rubbed in salt, and exchanging wedding rings, are led by an elder. After the ceremony, there is a wedding feast.

Many couples now wear Western-style clothing at these weddings. Also, since 1975, Vietnamese women do not change their last names after marriage. But children always take the last name of their father.

An important ingredient in Vietnamese cooking is *nuoc mam*, a fish sauce. *Nuoc mam* is a mixture of the salty juice from fermented fish, lime juice, garlic, chopped peppers, and sugar. Diners drizzle it over rice, drop it into soup, or use it for dipping spring rolls or pieces of meat. Other dipping sauces include a peanut sauce called *nuoc leo* and a spicy shrimp sauce called *mam tom*.

Ways of Dress

In cities, Vietnamese men often wear Western-style clothing, such as short-sleeved shirts and pants. Many Vietnamese women wear Western clothing, too. Pants suits or pants and blouses are common. Dresses are usually worn fairly long. It's common to see young people in the cities wearing jeans and T-shirts.

Outside the cities, most people wear traditional clothing. In rural areas of the north, women often dress in loose skirts and shirts. Men often wear coat-like garments that hang to their knees. In the south, people wear loose-fitting pants and long-sleeved shirts. Men and women wear sandals or go barefoot.

For special occasions, most women still wear the traditional two-piece garment called the *ao dai*. The top of the *ao dai* consists of a long-sleeved blouse with a high neckline. The blouse, which falls below the knees, has slits reaching to the waist on both sides. The top is worn over loose-fitting white or black pants. There is an *ao dai* for men as well, which has a shorter, looser top.

Hats are distinctive in Vietnam. The conical hat called the *non la* (meaning "leaf hat") is common. People wear the *non la* for protection against the hot sun or heavy rain. In the north,

These women wear the colorful headdresses of their ethnic group.

it is common to see many people wearing green canvas pith helmets, called *mucoi*, or French-style berets.

Modesty is very important for women. In rural areas especially, respectable women do not wear shorts, low-cut blouses, or short skirts.

The people of each tribal group have their own way of dressing. Men may wear Western-style garments, but women almost always wear traditional clothing. In the north, women of the Hmong tribe might be seen at open-air markets wearing dark blue or black clothing with large silver bracelets, necklaces, and earrings. Among the Red Zao people, women wear black pants and tunic tops decorated with colorful hand embroidery.

Wearing their school uniforms, this group of girls from a village in central Vietnam attend a Buddhist celebration.

4

SCHOOL AND RECREATION

Growing Up in Vietnam

The Vietnamese love children. Parents expect them to work hard at home and at school. A child's success brings honor to his or her entire family.

Busy School Days

All Vietnamese children between the ages of five and eleven must go to elementary school. There, they learn the basic skills of reading, writing, and mathematics. They also learn the importance of patriotism and service to their country.

Children with good grades may go on to secondary school. History, geography, literature, science, and a foreign language such as English or Russian are taught in secondary school. Those who do not go to secondary school might attend a technical school, where they learn skills in carpentry, mechanics, or agriculture. After secondary school, some students go on to college.

Before 1989, elementary and secondary school were free in Vietnam. Today, though, only the first three years of school are free. As a result, many parents can't afford to send their

47

children to school and the number of students in the higher grades has decreased.

Because the population is growing and there aren't enough new buildings, schools are overcrowded. Many Vietnamese children attend school in shifts. Some children go in the morning, from 7:00 to 11:15 A.M. Others attend in the afternoon, from 1:00 to 5:00 P.M. For most children, the school day begins with a walk from home—there are no school buses.

Teachers are strict in Vietnam. At the start of the day, they give oral tests. A student who answers a question wrong may have to write the correct answer dozens of times or stand in the corner until he or she figures it out.

Students go to school from September through May, Monday through Saturday. On Saturday, students stand in front of the class to recite what they have learned that week.

Students do not receive grades, such as As or Bs. Instead, each is ranked from first to last in the class. About once a month, the teacher sends a report to parents showing the child's rank and the subjects in which he or she needs to improve. At the end of the school year, the three students with the highest rank in each class earn prizes.

In addition to studying, students also take turns cleaning their school. Each student becomes part of a clean-up group at the start of the year. When it is a cleaning group's turn to work, the students arrive at school early. They sweep classrooms, wash blackboards, and throw out garbage.

The government and the Communist Party run all of the schools in Vietnam. Although the first few years of elementary school are free, parents must buy books and other supplies. If parents cannot afford the books, their children cannot start school at age five. Because some poor children must work to help their families, they may not go to school as early or as often as some other children.

Most Vietnamese children complete elementary school. But in rural areas, many children leave before the end of secondary school and go to work to help support their families. Even though most Vietnamese do not finish secondary school, about 93 percent of the people can read and write.

Fun and Games

Most students in elementary school don't play games during school hours. But during their free time children often swim, jump rope, or play games such as kickball, marbles, or

A group of boys gathers after school to play a favorite game—battledore.

hide-and-seek. They also enjoy card games. Battledore—kicking a shuttlecock with the foot to keep it in the air—is another popular pastime. Many boys take up martial arts like kung fu and karate.

Students who attend secondary school can play on sports teams. Soccer is the most popular sport. Students also join track, volleyball, tennis, and table-tennis teams.

In the evening, young people in cities meet to socialize on the street or in ice cream parlors. Some take music lessons or language courses. Dancing at discotheques and going to action movies are popular. So are karaoke lounges, places where people can sing along to recorded music. The Vietnamese also enjoy "café videos," where people sit at tables drinking soda or beer while watching videos.

In rural areas, people amuse themselves with ball-throwing, pigeon-flying, rice-cooking, and eel-catching contests. Playing chess and cards are popular activities, and so is playing a bamboo flute. Villagers also enjoy café videos or billiard tables set up in bamboo sheds.

Recreation for Everyone

People spend most of their free time with family and friends. Vietnam has beautiful beaches along its South China Sea coast, where many families enjoy relaxing together. The cool mountains near the city of Da Lat in the south are also popular for vacations.

Slow-motion shadow boxing, called *thai cuc quyen*, is a form of exercise enjoyed by the elderly and young women who want to keep in shape. *Thai cuc quyen* is related to Chinese kung fu. *Thai cuc quyen* and other exercises are done in public parks at sunrise.

One of the beautiful beaches along the South China Sea coast—a favorite Vietnamese vacation spot.

The government sponsors sports teams in the larger cities. Soccer is the team sport most popular with the public. The Vietnamese also enjoy contests in swimming, tennis, volleyball, badminton, table tennis, and handball.

51

Religious themes still interest modern artists in Vietnam.

5
THE ARTS

Ancient Arts Made New

Many of the beautiful arts practiced in Vietnam today were first introduced by the Chinese. Over the centuries, however, the Vietnamese have changed these art forms to produce works that are truly their own.

Beautiful Crafts

Many villages in the Red River Valley specialize in crafts such as ceramics, silk weaving, woodblock printing, and furniture carving with mother-of-pearl inlay. Most of these crafts were brought by the Chinese. However, the making of mother-of-pearl inlay is one of Vietnam's most original folk arts. It dates back more than 1,000 years. To make mother-of-pearl decoration, pieces of shell are glued to indented areas of wooden bowls, screens, trays, and furniture.

Lacquerware is an important craft that was brought to Vietnam by the Chinese in the 1400s. Artists first put ten coats of lacquer on a wooden object. Each coat is dried for a week, then sanded. Then they add the eleventh coat, which is

A woman weaves a blanket in the traditional pattern of her tribe.

a special lacquer that is sanded with a fine coal powder. Finally, the object is decorated with an engraving, painting, or mother-of-pearl inlay.

The art of painting on silk dates back to at least the 1200s in Vietnam. Silk painting was used before the days of photography to create pictures of people for ancestor worship. Today, if you visit some Buddhist temples, you can see fine silk paintings of famous people from Vietnam's past.

Music, Dance, and Theater

Like other arts, music in Vietnam has been influenced by China. For example, Vietnamese music is based on the Chinese pentatonic, or five-note, scale.

In general, there are three types of Vietnamese music: folk songs, classical music, and choral music. Folk songs

54

include children's songs, work songs, festival songs, and funeral songs. These are sung without instrumental accompaniment. Classical Vietnamese music is played by an orchestra of forty musicians. In the theater, instruments are used to accompany singing and dancing. Choral music, which is music meant to be sung by a choir, is especially interesting in Vietnam because the notes must correspond to the tones in spoken Vietnamese. The notes of a song cannot rise if the tone of the word being sung is falling.

Typical Vietnamese instruments include bamboo flutes and xylophones, the sixteen-string zither, and the double trumpet, which is made of two attached bamboo tubes. Skin drums, gongs, and cymbals are also important. The *dan bau* is a unique Vietnamese instrument. It has one copper string stretched across a large gourd. The sound of the *dan bau* mimics the tones of the Vietnamese language.

The Vietnamese enjoy classical theater, which is called *hat tuong* in the north and *hat boi* in the south. It is based on Chinese opera and is performed with six musicians. The audience can tell a lot about the characters in *hat tuong* by looking at their makeup and costumes. A character with red face paint, for instance, is brave. One with a white face is cruel. Green-faced characters come from the lowlands. Those with black faces come from the highlands. Male characters stroke their beards in different ways to show feelings such as worry or anger.

Puppetry is a special Vietnamese tradition. Regular puppet shows are called *roi can*. Water puppetry, or *roi nuoc*, is a uniquely Vietnamese art. *Roi nuoc* takes place outdoors, on the surface of a lake or pool. The puppets seem to glide on the water, acting out folktales, historical events, and stories

Two pairs of hands work to bring this richly dressed puppet to life.

about village life. Puppeteers stand in water behind a bamboo curtain and move the puppets with hidden bamboo poles attached to strings and pulleys. The puppets are made of carved wood painted with lacquer. The characters include fishermen, emperors, heroes, animals, and water dragons.

Storytelling and Writing

There are many Vietnamese folktales that have been passed down by word of mouth from generation to generation. These tales include stories about animals, religious figures like the Buddha, and famous people from Vietnamese history. Many have a lesson to teach.

The most popular form of Vietnamese literature has always been poetry. Novels became popular during the years of French rule. People still enjoy reading them, especially in the south. However, the government carefully controls the books that people are allowed to read.

A Changing Architecture

Much of Vietnam's traditional architecture no longer exists. When the French ruled, they knocked down many Vietnamese structures and put up their own buildings in their place. Many buildings were also destroyed during the Vietnam War. And other buildings, made of wood, have been damaged by the moist tropical climate.

Interesting sculpture can still be found, though, in temples, pagodas, and tombs. Figures of dragons or demons decorate the rooftops of Buddhist temples. Statues of sacred animals from Vietnamese and Chinese mythology line the walls of pagodas. The animals are there to guard the pagodas and to bring good luck. For example, dragons symbolize power, while turtles stand for long life. Some pagodas also contain sandalwood or bronze statues of the Buddha.

In the southern part of Vietnam one can see many graceful brick towers and carved sandstone figures left behind by the Chams.

Vietnam is a beautiful land with a long history of traditions. The Vietnamese, despite their many struggles, continue to honor the ancient customs and ways of their forefathers.

The National Theater is one of Hanoi's many beautiful buildings.

Country Facts

Official Name: *Cong Hoa Xa Hoi Chu Nghia Viet Nam* (Socialist Republic of Vietnam)

Capital: Hanoi

Location: in Southeast Asia on the eastern edge of the Indochina Peninsula. Bordered on the north by China, on the west by Laos and Cambodia, on the south by the Gulf of Thailand, and on the east by the South China Sea and the Gulf of Tonkin.

Area: 127,207 square miles (329,465 square kilometers). *Greatest distances:* east–west: 380 miles (612 kilometers); north–south: 1,030 miles (1,657 kilometers). *Coastline:* 1,440 miles (2,317 kilometers)

Elevation: *Highest:* Phan Si Pan, at 10,308 feet (3,142 kilometers); *Lowest:* sea level along the coast.

Climate: largely tropical and wet. The climate is influenced by elevation and by seasonal monsoons.

Population: 76.6 million. *Distribution:* 20% urban; 80% rural.

Form of Government: a Communist dictatorship

Important Products: *Agriculture:* rice, corn, sweet potatoes, cassavas, pulse plants, sugarcane, cotton, tea, coffee, and tobacco. *Industries:* machine tools, iron and steel, fertilizer. *Natural resources:* tropical hardwoods, fish and shellfish, coal, tin, chrome, and phosphate.

Basic Unit of Money: dong; 1 dong = 10 hao = 100 xu

Languages: The official language is Vietnamese; others spoken include French, Chinese, English, Khmer, and various tribal languages.

Religion: Buddhism is the main religion, but other religions and philosophies, such as Taoism, Confucianism, Roman Catholicism, Cao Dai, Hoa Hao, Islam, and animism, are also practiced.

National Anthem: *Tien Quan Ca* ("Marching to the Front")

Flag: red field with a gold star in the center

Major Holidays: New Year's Day (*Tet Duong Lich*), January 1; the lunar New Year (*Tet Nguyen Dan*, or *Tet*), late January to mid-February; the anniversary of the founding of the Vietnamese Communist Party (*Thanh Lap Dang CSVN*), February 3; Trung Sisters Day, celebrating two heroes (*Hai Ba Trung*), March; Liberation Day, celebrating the unification of Vietnam (*Saigon Giai*

Phong), April 30; International Workers' Day (*Quoc Te Lao Dong*), May 1; Ho Chi Minh's birthday (*Sinh Nhat Bac Ho*), May 19; Wandering Souls Day (*Trung Nguyen*), mid-summer; National Day, celebrating the first reading of the Declaration of Independence of the Democratic Republic of Vietnam by Ho Chi Minh (*Quoc Khanh*), September 2; Children's Festival (*Tet Trung Thu*), mid-September.

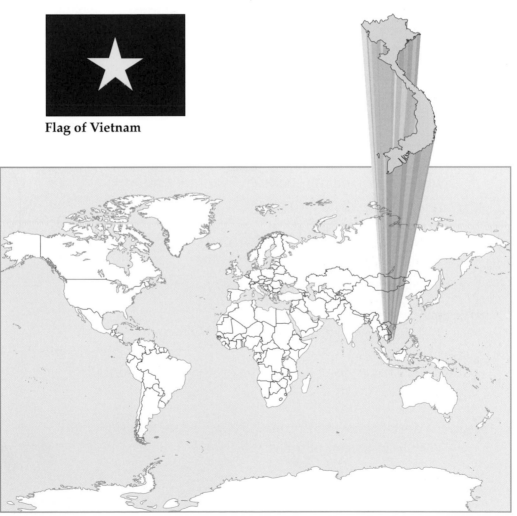

Flag of Vietnam

Vietnam in the World

Glossary

communism: a system of government in which all property and goods are owned by the government and are supposed to be shared equally by the people

delta: an area of fertile soil deposited by a river at its mouth. Most deltas are shaped in the form of a triangle.

emperor: a royal ruler, similar to a king

ethnic group: a group of people who share the same language and culture

gender: sex; whether a person is female or male

missionary: a person who is sent by a religious group to spread the religion and promote goodwill in another country

monsoon: a seasonal wind that blows over the Indian Ocean and southern Asia and brings heavy rains

pagoda: a tower in a Buddhist temple

rain forest: a dense forest in an area of very heavy rainfall

ravine: a deep narrow valley, usually carved by flowing water over a very long period of time

rice paddy: a flooded field used for growing rice

tropical climate: a climate that is hot year-round. Places with a tropical climate are located in the tropics, the region of earth near the equator.

typhoon: a violent windstorm in the Indian and western Pacific Oceans. In the Atlantic Ocean, these storms are called hurricanes.

Western: referring to the people and customs of Europe and North America

For Further Reading

Cole, Wendy M. *Vietnam*. New York: Chelsea House Publishers, 1989.

Garland, Sherry. *Vietnam: Rebuilding a Nation*. Minneapolis, Minnesota: Dillon Press, Inc., 1990.

Hartz, Paula R. *Taoism*. New York: Facts On File, 1993.

Hoobler, Thomas and Dorothy. *Confucianism*. New York: Facts On File, 1993.

Norland, Patricia. *Vietnam*. Milwaukee, Wisconsin: Gareth Stevens Children's Books, 1991.

Seah, Audrey. *Vietnam*. New York: Marshall Cavendish, 1993.

Vietnam...in Pictures. Minneapolis, Minnesota: Lerner Publications Company, 1994.

Wangu, Madhu Bazaz. *Buddhism*. New York: Facts On File, 1993.

Index

About the Author

Olivia Skelton writes frequently for children. She has published magazine articles, books, and educational texts. She specializes in geography, history, and science, and she maintains a keen interest in the development of world cultures. Ms. Skelton lives in central New Jersey.